JUST **100** CALORIES

JUST **100** CALORIES

Love Food™ is an imprint of
Parragon Books Ltd

Parragon
Queen Street House
4 Queen Street
Bath BA1 1HE, UK

Love Food™ and the accompanying heart
device is a trademark of Parragon Books Ltd

Design: Terry Jeavons & Company
Photographer: Mike Cooper
Home economist: Lincoln Jefferson

ISBN 978-1-4054-8779-5

Printed in China

This book uses imperial, metric, or US cup
measurements. Follow the same units of
measurement throughout; do not mix imperial
and metric. All spoon measurements are
level, unless otherwise stated: teaspoons
are assumed to be 5ml, and tablespoons
are assumed to be 15ml. Unless otherwise
stated, milk is assumed to be whole, eggs
and individual fruits such as bananas are
medium, and pepper is freshly ground
black pepper.

Recipes using raw or very lightly cooked eggs
should be avoided by children, the elderly,
pregnant women, convalescents, and anyone
suffering from an illness. Pregnant and
breast-feeding women are advised to avoid
eating peanuts and peanut products.

Contents

Introduction

Today's lifestyle is not conducive to healthy eating. It is all too easy to snack on convenience foods, especially when on the move. Bingeing when you are starving-hungry is the classic way to pile on the pounds and, before you know where you are, you are far larger than you would wish to be. But how can this change? There is a host of diet books on the market, each one promising that it has the answer—low carbohydrate, high protein, microbiotic, or Glycemic Index (GI). So, we lurch from one diet to another in a desperate struggle to get on top of the problem. We all know that to enjoy a balanced diet we need to cut out the fat and to eat lots of fruit, vegetables, and fiber. But what does that mean, and how do we know if we are achieving this?

The simple fact is that the more calories that are consumed, the greater the amount of food that is stored in the body as fat, no matter where those excess calories come from. In the West we tend to eat far too many calories—for most healthy women the daily requirement is no more than 2,000 calories, while healthy men require no more than 2,500 calories per day (this does not apply to manual workers). In order to lose weight you have to reduce the amount of calories consumed. The recommended daily amount of calories for women in order to lose weight is 1,500 and for men it is 2,000. Any balanced weight loss program should also include regular exercise.

Children, because they are growing and are often far more active than adults, require a good proportion of their calories from high energy-giving foods, such as slow-releasing complex carbohydrates like vegetables, fruits, beans, and whole wheat products, plus, of course, a good proportion of protein, including fish, poultry, and lean meat, and also a certain amount of products containing fat. All these foods contain important minerals such as calcium, which is vital for growth. As we grow older, the body's metabolism slows down and so fewer calories are required. The one to watch is fat. This contains twice as many calories as any other food. One gram of carbohydrate or protein is 4 calories while 1 gram of fat is 9 calories.

This book is designed in a practical way to stop the yo-yo effect of weight loss and weight gain, with recipes that are calorie-counted, so you can see at a glance exactly how many calories there are in each portion. Each delicious recipe is easy to prepare and cook and will help you control your intake and maintain a balanced diet. There are some spicy fish dishes, exotic chicken meals as well as some favorite meat recipes but, don't despair, if you have a sweet tooth there are a few little gems together with some healthy drinks, and the occasional treat of a glass or two of cheer. So get counting and cooking and see how easy it is to maintain a healthy and balanced diet.

1 Breakfast & Brunches

There are plenty of recipes within this chapter to tempt and delight without piling on the pounds, ranging from Melon & Strawberry Crunch, a delicious start to any morning and is simply bursting with fruit, to Smoked Salmon Scramble or tasty Hot Garlic-Stuffed Mushrooms, perfect for a lazy Sunday brunch.

Melon & Strawberry Crunch

INGREDIENTS

serves 4
calories per
portion

98

not including
orange juice
or milk

⅓ cup rolled oats

¼ cup oat bran

2 tbsp toasted slivered almonds

scant ¼ cup plumped dried apricots, finely chopped

½ melon, such as galia

8 oz/225 g strawberries

⅔ cup orange juice or lowfat milk, to serve (optional)

1 Put the rolled oats and oat bran in a bowl and stir in the almonds and dried apricots.

2 Discard the skin and seeds from the melon and cut into small bite-size pieces. Halve the strawberries if large.

3 Divide the rolled oat mixture among 4 individual bowls then top with the fruits. If liked, serve with either lowfat milk or orange juice.

Asparagus with Tomato & Bacon

serves 4
calories per
portion

74

INGREDIENTS

12 oz/350 g fresh asparagus
spears

four 4 oz/115 g slices lean
Canadian bacon or 4 thin
slices prosciutto

4 medium tomatoes

pepper

1 Trim off the woody part of the asparagus stems and discard. Using a vegetable peeler, peel the spears in a downward action to remove any other woody parts.

2 Bring a large skillet half-filled with water to a boil (or use a steamer). Add the asparagus to the boiling water and cook for 5 to 6 minutes, or until tender. Drain and keep warm.

3 Meanwhile, preheat the broiler and line the broiler rack with foil. Put the bacon slices on the foil-lined broiler rack. Cut the tomatoes in half and place these on the broiler rack. Broil for 4 to 5 minutes, or until the bacon is crisp. Turn the bacon over halfway through cooking. If using prosciutto, there is no need to cook it.

4 Divide the asparagus, bacon, and tomatoes among 4 plates. To serve, sprinkle the tomatoes with pepper, to taste.

Grapefruit Cups

INGREDIENTS

serves 4
calories
per half

78

2 red or pink grapefruit, about
1 lb/450 g each

2 tbsp raw brown sugar

2 ripe passion fruit or 2 tbsp
orange flower water

1 Preheat the broiler to medium and line the broiler rack with foil. Cut the grapefruits in half and, using a grapefruit knife or small, sharp-pointed knife, carefully loosen the segments and remove the central piece of pith. Carefully cut under the segments to make them easier to remove.

2 Put the grapefruit on the foil-lined rack and sprinkle with the sugar. Cook under the broiler for 5 minutes, or until the sugar has melted.

3 If using passion fruit, scoop out the seeds and flesh, and spoon over the cooked grapefruit. Alternatively, pour over the orange flower water. Serve half a grapefruit per person while still hot.

Wake-Up Kabobs

INGREDIENTS

serves 4
calories per
kabob

61

½ red apple, cored and sliced

1 large banana, peeled and cut into bite-size pieces

1 tbsp orange or lemon juice

1 large watermelon wedge, peeled, seeded, and cut into small chunks

1 melon wedge, such as ogen or galia, peeled, seeded, and cut into small chunks

8 fresh strawberries

2 tsp honey

1 Preheat the broiler to high and line the broiler rack with foil. Brush the apple and banana with the orange juice.

2 Thread the melon, apple, banana, and strawberries onto 4 kabob sticks or presoaked wooden skewers and place on the broiler rack.

3 Drizzle with the honey then broil for 5 to 6 minutes, turning the kabobs over halfway through cooking. Serve while warm.

Oven-Baked Eggs with Tomato Salsa

INGREDIENTS

serves 4
calories per
portion

93

FOR THE SALSA

2 ripe tomatoes, finely
chopped

3 scallions, trimmed
and finely chopped

1-inch/2.5-cm piece cucumber,
finely chopped

Tabasco sauce, to taste

1 tbsp chopped fresh cilantro

FOR THE EGGS

4 sprays olive oil

4 eggs

pepper

1 Preheat the oven to 350°F/180°C. To prepare the salsa, put the tomatoes, scallions, cucumber, and Tabasco sauce in a small pan and set aside.

2 Lightly spray 4 ramekins with oil and place a spoonful of the prepared salsa in the base of each dish. Carefully break an egg into each ramekin dish. Place the dishes in a roasting pan half-filled with hot water and sprinkle the top of each egg with pepper. Heat the remaining salsa in the pan gently.

3 Bake the eggs for 8 to 12 minutes, or until cooked to personal preference. Stir the chopped cilantro into the reserved salsa and serve with the cooked eggs.

Smoked Salmon Scramble

INGREDIENTS

serves 4

calories per portion

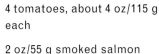

92

4 tomatoes, about 4 oz/115 g each

2 oz/55 g smoked salmon pieces

2 eggs

1 egg white

1 tbsp water

pepper

1 tbsp snipped fresh chives, for sprinkling

1 Preheat the broiler to high and line the broiler rack with foil. Cut the tomatoes in half and scoop out the flesh and seeds. Chop the flesh finely then place in a strainer to allow the excess liquid to drain away.

2 Cut the smoked salmon into small pieces. In a separate bowl, beat the eggs, egg white, and water, with pepper to taste. Heat a nonstick small pan and when hot, add the beaten egg. Cook for 1 minute, stirring continuously, then stir in the drained tomato flesh and the smoked salmon. Continue to cook, stirring for 3 to 4 minutes, or until the eggs are set to personal preference.

3 Meanwhile, place the halved tomatoes on the broiler rack and broil for 2 minutes. When the egg mixture is set, use to fill the warm tomato shells. Sprinkle with snipped chives and serve two tomato cups per person.

Hot Garlic-Stuffed Mushrooms

INGREDIENTS

serves 4
calories per
mushroom

4 large portobello mushrooms

4 sprays olive oil

2–3 garlic cloves, crushed

2 shallots

½ cup fresh whole wheat
breadcrumbs

few fresh basil sprigs

scant ¼ cup plumped dried
apricots, chopped

1 tbsp pine nuts

2 oz/55 g feta cheese

pepper

1 Preheat the oven to 350°F/180°C. Remove the stalks from the mushrooms and set aside. Spray the bases of the mushrooms with the oil and place undersides up in a roasting pan.

2 Put the mushroom stalks in a food processor with the garlic, shallots, and breadcrumbs. Set aside a few basil sprigs for the garnish then place the remainder in the food processor with the apricots, pine nuts, and feta cheese. Add pepper to taste.

3 Process for 1 to 2 minutes, or until a stuffing consistency is formed, then divide among the mushroom caps.

4 Bake for 10 to 12 minutes, or until the mushrooms are tender and the stuffing is crisp on the top. Serve garnished with the reserved basil sprigs.

Zucchini, Carrot & Tomato Frittata

serves 4
calories per
portion

100

INGREDIENTS

2 sprays olive oil

1 onion, cut into small wedges

1–2 garlic cloves, crushed

2 eggs

2 egg whites

1 zucchini, about 3 oz/85 g, trimmed and grated

2 carrots, about 4 oz/115 g, peeled and grated

2 tomatoes, chopped

pepper

1 tbsp shredded fresh basil, for sprinkling

1 Heat the oil in a large nonstick skillet, add the onion and garlic, and sauté for 5 minutes, stirring frequently. Beat the eggs and egg whites together in a bowl then pour into the skillet. Using a spatula or fork, pull the egg mixture from the sides of the skillet into the center.

2 Once the base has set lightly, add the grated zucchini and carrots with the tomatoes. Add pepper to taste and continue to cook over low heat until the eggs are set to personal preference.

3 Sprinkle with the shredded basil and cut the frittata into quarters. Serve one quarter per person.

Crisp Bread Bruschetta

serves 4
calories per
crisp bread

81

INGREDIENTS

4 crisp breads

2 tsp lowfat herb-flavored cream cheese

2 oz/55 g arugula

½ small melon, such as ogen or galia

1 oz/25 g seedless grapes

2 cherry tomatoes (optional)

3 oz/85 g lean boiled ham, thinly sliced (optional)

4 raspberries (optional)

4 thin slices peeled cucumber (optional)

¼ small apple, thinly sliced (optional)

pepper

1 Spread the crisp breads with the lowfat cream cheese and top with the arugula.

2 Discard the seeds and skin from the melon and cut into tiny wedges. Arrange on top of the arugula and arrange the grapes on top. Sprinkle with pepper and serve. You can vary the toppings using the cherry tomatoes, ham, raspberries, and thin slices of cucumber and apple, for example.

Filo-Wrapped Asparagus

INGREDIENTS

serves 4
calories per
portion

96

FOR THE DIP

⅓ cup natural cottage cheese

1 tbsp lowfat milk

4 scallions, trimmed
and finely chopped

2 tbsp chopped fresh mixed
herbs, such as basil, mint,
and tarragon

pepper

FOR THE ASPARAGUS

20 asparagus spears

5 sheets filo dough

lemon wedges, to serve

1 Preheat the oven to 375°F/190°C. To make the dip, put the cottage cheese in a bowl and add the milk. Beat until smooth then stir in the scallions, chopped herbs, and pepper to taste. Place in a serving bowl, cover lightly, and chill in the refrigerator until required.

2 Cut off and discard the woody end of the asparagus and shave with a vegetable peeler to remove any woody parts from the spears.

3 Cut the filo dough into quarters and place one sheet on a clean counter. Brush lightly with water then place a spear at one end. Roll up to encase the spear, and place on a large baking sheet. Repeat until all the asparagus spears are wrapped in dough.

4 Bake for 10 to 12 minutes, or until the dough is golden. Serve 5 spears per person with lemon wedges and the dip (a quarter per person) on the side.

Pepper & Basil Pots

serves 4
calories per
pot

69

INGREDIENTS

1 tsp olive oil

2 shallots, finely chopped

2 garlic cloves, crushed

pepper

2 red bell peppers, peeled,
seeded, and sliced
into strips

1 orange bell pepper, peeled,
seeded, and sliced
into strips

4 tomatoes, thinly sliced

2 tbsp shredded fresh basil

salad greens, to serve

1 Lightly brush 4 ramekin dishes with the oil.
Mix the shallots and garlic together in a bowl
and season with pepper to taste.

2 Layer the red and orange bell peppers with
the tomatoes in the prepared ramekin dishes,
sprinkling each layer with the shallot mixture
and shredded basil. When all the ingredients
have been added, cover lightly with plastic
wrap or parchment paper. Weigh down using
small weights and leave in the refrigerator for
at least 6 hours, or preferably overnight.

3 When ready to serve, remove the weights
and carefully run a knife around the edges.
Invert onto serving plates and serve with
salad greens.

Mushroom Pâté

INGREDIENTS

serves 4
calories per
portion

61

not including
crisp breads

scant ¼ cup dried porcini
mushrooms

1 tsp olive oil

2 shallots, finely chopped

2 garlic cloves, crushed

1 fresh jalapeño chile, seeded
and finely chopped

2 celery stalks, trimmed and
finely chopped

8 oz/225 g closed cup
mushrooms, wiped and sliced

grated rind and juice of
1 orange

½ cup fresh breadcrumbs

1 tbsp chopped fresh parsley

1 small egg, beaten

pepper

TO SERVE
raw vegetable sticks
crisp breads

1 Preheat the oven to 350°F/180°C. Put the dried mushrooms in a bowl and cover with freshly boiled water. Let soak for 30 minutes then drain, chop, and set aside.

2 Heat the oil in a medium heavy-bottom pan, then add the shallots, garlic, chile, and celery. Cook, stirring frequently for 3 minutes, then add both the dried and fresh mushrooms and cook for an additional 2 minutes.

3 Add the orange juice and continue to cook for 3 to 4 minutes, or until the mushrooms have collapsed. Remove the pan from the heat and stir in the orange rind, breadcrumbs, parsley, beaten egg, and pepper to taste. Mix well.

4 Spoon the mixture into 4 individual ramekin dishes and level the surfaces. Place the dishes in a small baking pan and pour enough water to come halfway up the sides of the ramekins.

5 Cook for 15 to 20 minutes, or until a skewer inserted in the center of each ramekin comes out clean. Remove and either let stand for 10 minutes before serving warm or chill until ready to serve. Turn out and serve with vegetable sticks and crisp breads.

Spicy Stuffed Peppers

INGREDIENTS

serves 4
calories per
pepper

93

4 assorted colored bell peppers

3 sprays olive oil

1 onion, finely chopped

2 garlic cloves, chopped

1-inch/2.5-cm piece fresh ginger, peeled and grated

1–2 fresh serrano chiles, seeded and chopped

1 tsp ground cumin

1 tsp ground coriander

scant ½ cup cooked brown basmati rice

1 large carrot, about 4 oz/115 g, peeled and grated

1 large zucchini, about 3 oz/ 85 g, trimmed and grated

scant ¼ cup plumped dried apricots, finely chopped

1 tbsp chopped fresh cilantro

pepper

⅔ cup water

fresh herbs, to garnish

1 Preheat the oven to 375°F/190°C. Cut the tops off the bell peppers and set aside. Discard the seeds from each pepper. Place the peppers in a large bowl and cover with boiling water. Let soak for 10 minutes then drain and set aside.

2 Heat a nonstick skillet and spray with the oil. Add the onion, garlic, ginger, and chiles and sauté for 3 minutes, stirring frequently. Sprinkle in the ground spices and continue to cook for an additional 2 minutes.

3 Remove the skillet from the heat and stir in the rice, carrot, zucchini, apricots, chopped cilantro, and pepper to taste. Stir well, then use to stuff the peppers.

4 Place the stuffed peppers in an ovenproof dish large enough to allow the peppers to stand upright. Put the reserved tops in position. Pour the water around their bases, cover loosely with the lid or foil, and cook for 25 to 30 minutes, or until piping hot. Serve garnished with herbs.

Open Rösti Omelet

serves 4
calories per
portion

99

INGREDIENTS

2 oz/55 g old potatoes,
peeled and grated

1 onion, grated

2 garlic cloves, crushed

1 carrot, about 4 oz/115 g,
peeled and grated

4 sprays olive oil

1 yellow bell pepper, peeled
and thinly sliced

1 zucchini, about 3 oz/85 g,
trimmed and thinly sliced

3 oz/85 g cherry tomatoes,
halved

2 eggs

3 egg whites

pepper

1 tbsp snipped fresh chives

fresh arugula, to garnish

1 Put the grated potatoes into a large bowl and cover with cold water. Leave for 15 minutes then drain, rinse thoroughly, and dry on absorbent paper towels or a clean dishtowel. Mix with the grated onion, garlic, and carrot.

2 Heat a heavy-bottom nonstick skillet and spray with the oil. Add the potato, onion, garlic, and carrot mixture and cook over low heat for 5 minutes, pressing the vegetables down firmly with a spatula. Add the peeled bell pepper and zucchini slices. Cover with a lid or crumpled piece of foil and cook very gently, stirring occasionally, for 5 minutes.

3 Add the halved cherry tomatoes and cook for an additional 2 minutes, or until the vegetables are tender.

4 Beat the whole eggs, egg whites, pepper to taste, and the chives together in a bowl. Pour over the vegetable mixture and cook for 4 to 5 minutes, stirring the egg from the sides of the skillet toward the center, until the vegetables are tender and the eggs are set. Serve immediately, a quarter per person, garnished with arugula leaves.

2 Light Lunches & Snacks

Soups are a great idea for lunch or when a light snack is required, and in this chapter there are some super recipes. Try the deliciously warming Sweet Potato & Garlic Soup, or a salad—such as Spicy Warm Crab Salad or Fruity Cottage Cheese Salad, all guaranteed to please.

Herby Vegetable Soup

INGREDIENTS

serves 4
calories per
portion

98

2 sprays olive oil

1 onion, chopped

2 carrots, about 4 oz/115 g,
peeled and chopped

2 celery stalks, trimmed
and sliced

1 potato, about 2 oz/55 g,
peeled and chopped

scant ¼ cup quick-cook pearl
barley

3½ cups vegetable stock

1 bouquet garni

pepper

⅔ cup lowfat milk

1 tbsp chopped fresh mixed
herbs, such as parsley, chives,
and oregano

2 tbsp lowfat plain yogurt,
to serve

1 Heat a large pan and spray with the oil. Add the onion, carrots, celery, and potato and cook over low heat, stirring frequently, for 5 minutes. Rinse the pearl barley then add to the pan together with the stock and bouquet garni and pepper to taste.

2 Bring to a boil, reduce the heat to a simmer, cover with a lid, and simmer for 15 minutes, or until the vegetables are tender. Discard the bouquet garni, stir in the milk, and heat gently for 3 minutes. Stir in the chopped herbs and adjust the seasoning, if necessary. Divide equally among 4 warmed bowls with a spoonful of yogurt swirled around in each.

Speedy Minestrone Soup

INGREDIENTS

serves 4
calories per
portion

2 sprays olive oil

1 onion, finely chopped

1 large carrot, about 4 oz/115 g,
peeled and diced

2 celery stalks, trimmed and
sliced

1 bouquet garni

14 oz/400 g canned chopped
tomatoes

2 oz/55 g dried soup pasta
shells or spaghetti broken into
small lengths

3½ cups vegetable stock

½ small cabbage, about
8 oz/225 g

pepper

1 Heat the oil in a large pan, add the onion,
carrot, and celery and sauté gently for
5 minutes, stirring frequently. Add the bouquet
garni with the chopped tomatoes. Half-fill
the empty tomato can with water, swirl to
remove all the remaining tomatoes, then pour
into the pan.

2 Add the pasta with the stock and bring
to a boil. Reduce the heat to a simmer and
cook for 12 minutes, or until the vegetables
are almost tender.

3 Discard any outer leaves and hard central
core from the cabbage and shred. Wash well,
then add to the pan with pepper to taste.
Continue to cook for 5 to 8 minutes, or until all
the vegetables are tender, but still firm to
the bite. Serve divided equally among 4
warmed bowls.

Parsnip & Broccoli Soup

INGREDIENTS

serves 4
calories per
portion

2 sprays olive oil

1 onion, chopped

10½ oz/300 g parsnips, peeled and chopped

3½ cups vegetable stock

10½ oz/300 g broccoli florets

pepper

⅓ cup fresh or frozen corn kernels

1 oz/25 g bleu cheese, such as St Agur or Roquefort

1 Heat the oil in a large pan, add the onion and parsnips, and sauté for 5 minutes, stirring frequently. Add the stock, bring to a boil, cover with a lid, and reduce the heat to a simmer. Cook for 10 minutes.

2 Meanwhile, trim the broccoli, discarding any woody stalks, and cut into small florets. Use the tender parts of the stalk as well as the florets. Add to the pan and continue to cook for an additional 5 to 8 minutes, or until the vegetables are tender.

3 Let cool slightly then pass through a food processor to form a purée and return to the pan. Season with pepper to taste and add the corn and bleu cheese. Heat gently, stirring occasionally, for about 5 minutes, or until the corn is tender and the cheese has melted. Serve piping hot, divided equally among 4 warmed bowls.

Miso Fish Soup

INGREDIENTS

serves 4
calories per
portion

98

3½ cups fish stock or
vegetable stock

1-inch/2.5-cm piece fresh
ginger, peeled and grated

1 tbsp mirin or dry sherry

1 fresh Thai chile, seeded and
finely sliced

1 carrot, about 3 oz/85 g,
peeled and thinly sliced

2 oz/55 g daikon, peeled and
cut into thin strips or ½ bunch
radishes, trimmed and sliced

1 yellow bell pepper, seeded
and cut into thin strips

3 oz/85 g shiitake mushrooms,
sliced if large

1½ oz/40 g thread egg noodles

8 oz/225 g sole fillets, skinned
and cut into strips

1 tbsp miso paste

4 scallions, trimmed
and shredded

1 Pour the stock into a large pan and add the ginger, mirin, and chile. Bring to a boil then reduce the heat and simmer for 5 minutes.

2 Add the carrot with the daikon, bell pepper strips, mushrooms, and noodles and simmer for an additional 3 minutes.

3 Add the fish strips with the miso paste and continue to cook for 2 minutes, or until the fish is tender. Divide equally among 4 serving bowls, top with the scallions and serve.

Sweet Potato & Garlic Soup

INGREDIENTS

serves 4
calories per
portion

1 whole garlic bulb

2 sprays olive oil

1 onion, chopped

10½ oz/300 g sweet potatoes, peeled and chopped

4 cups vegetable stock

4 oz/115 g green string beans, trimmed and finely chopped

pepper

4 tbsp lowfat plain yogurt

1 tbsp snipped fresh chives

1 Preheat the oven to 375°F/190°C. Pull the garlic bulb apart and put in a small roasting pan. Roast in the oven for 20 minutes, or until soft. Remove and let cool before squeezing out the soft insides. Set aside.

2 Heat the oil in a heavy-bottom pan, add the onion and sweet potato, and cook, stirring continuously, for 5 minutes. Add the stock and bring to a boil. Cover with a lid, reduce the heat, and simmer for 10 minutes. Add the green string beans and the roasted garlic flesh and continue to simmer for 10 minutes, or until the potatoes are tender. Remove and let cool slightly.

3 Set aside 2 tablespoons of the cooked green beans, then pass the soup through a food processor and return to the rinsed-out pan. Add the reserved beans with pepper to taste and heat through for 3 minutes.

4 Divide equally among 4 warmed serving bowls, swirl a spoonful of yogurt in each, and sprinkle with snipped chives. Serve immediately.

Warm Salmon & Mango Salad

INGREDIENTS

serves 4
calories per
portion

4 oz/115 g sungold or red
cherry tomatoes

3 oz/85 g salmon fillets,
skinned and cut into small
cubes

1 large ripe mango (about
5 oz/140 g peeled fruit), peeled
and cut into small chunks

2 tbsp orange juice

1 tbsp soy sauce

4 oz/115 g assorted salad
greens

½ cucumber, trimmed and
sliced into thin sticks

6 scallions, trimmed
and chopped

FOR THE DRESSING

4 tbsp lowfat plain yogurt

1 tsp soy sauce

1 tbsp finely grated orange
rind

1 Cut half the tomatoes in half and set aside.

2 Thread the salmon with the whole tomatoes and half the mango chunks onto 4 kabob sticks. Mix the orange juice and soy sauce together in a small bowl and brush over the kabobs. Let marinate for 15 minutes, brushing with the remaining orange juice mixture at least once more.

3 Arrange the salad greens on a serving platter with the reserved halved tomatoes, mango chunks, the cucumber sticks, and scallions.

4 Preheat the broiler to high and line the broiler rack with foil. To make the dressing, mix the yogurt, soy sauce, and grated orange rind together in a small bowl and set aside.

5 Place the salmon kabobs on the broiler rack, brush again with the marinade, and broil for 5 to 7 minutes, or until the salmon is cooked. Turn the kabobs over halfway through cooking and brush with any remaining marinade.

6 Divide the prepared salad among 4 plates, top each with a kabob, and then drizzle with the dressing.

Fruity Cottage Cheese Salad

INGREDIENTS

serves 4
calories per
portion

⅓ cup cottage cheese

1 tsp chopped fresh parsley

1 tbsp snipped fresh chives

1 tsp chopped fresh chervil
or basil

2 assorted colored bell
peppers, seeded and peeled

1 small melon, such as ogen
(about 10½ oz/300 g after
peeling and seeding)

6 oz/175 g assorted salad
greens

2 oz/55 g seedless grapes

1 red onion, thinly sliced

FOR THE DRESSING

3 tbsp freshly squeezed lime
juice

1 small fresh red chile, seeded
and finely chopped

1 tsp honey

1 tbsp soy sauce

1 Place the cottage cheese in a bowl and stir in the chopped herbs. Cover lightly and set aside.

2 Cut the peeled bell peppers into thin strips and set aside. Cut the melon in half, discard the seeds and cut into small wedges. Remove and discard the rind, or run a sharp knife between the skin and flesh to loosen, then cut the flesh horizontally across. Push the flesh in alternate directions but so that it still sits on the skin. Set aside.

3 Arrange the salad greens on a large serving platter with the melon wedges.

4 Spoon the herb-flavored cottage cheese on the platter and arrange the reserved bell peppers, the grapes, and red onion slices around the cheese.

5 To make the dressing, mix the lime juice, chile, honey, and soy sauce together in a small bowl or pitcher then drizzle over the salad and serve as 4 portions.

Spicy Warm Crab Salad

serves 4
calories per
portion

INGREDIENTS

2 sprays sunflower oil

1 fresh serrano chile, seeded
and finely chopped

4 oz/115 g snow peas, cut
diagonally in half

6 scallions, trimmed
and finely shredded

2 heaping tbsp frozen corn
kernels

5½ oz/150 g white crabmeat,
drained if canned

2 oz/55 g peeled raw shrimp,
thawed if frozen

1 carrot, about 3 oz/85 g,
peeled and grated

¾ cup bean sprouts

8 oz/225 g fresh baby
spinach leaves

1 tbsp finely grated
orange rind

2 tbsp orange juice

1 tbsp chopped fresh cilantro,
for sprinkling

1 Heat a wok and when hot, spray in the oil
and heat for 30 seconds. Add the chile and
snow peas then stir-fry over medium heat
for 2 minutes.

2 Add the scallions and corn and continue to
stir-fry for an additional 1 minute.

3 Add the crabmeat, shrimp, grated carrot,
bean sprouts, and spinach leaves. Stir in the
orange rind and juice and stir-fry for 2 to
3 minutes, or until the spinach has begun to
wilt and everything is cooked. Serve divided
equally among 4 bowls, sprinkled with the
chopped cilantro.

Warm Asian-Style Salad

INGREDIENTS

serves 4
calories per
portion

98

4 oz/115 g broccoli florets

4 oz/115 g baby carrots, scraped and cut in half lengthwise

5 oz/140 g bok choy

2 sprays sunflower oil

1 red onion, sliced

1–2 fresh Thai chiles, seeded and sliced

1-inch/2.5-cm fresh ginger, peeled and grated

2 whole star anise

1 red bell pepper, seeded and cut into strips

1 orange bell pepper, seeded and cut into strips

4 oz/115 g baby zucchini, trimmed and sliced diagonally

4 oz/115 g baby corn, sliced in half lengthwise

2 tbsp orange juice

1 tbsp soy sauce

1 tbsp cashew nuts

1 Cut the broccoli into tiny florets then bring a small pan of water to a boil and add the halved carrots. Cook for 3 minutes then add the broccoli and cook for an additional 2 minutes. Drain and plunge into cold water then drain again and set aside.

2 Arrange 1 oz/25 g of bok choy on a large serving platter. Shred the remainder and set aside.

3 Heat a wok and when hot, add the oil and heat for 30 seconds. Add the sliced onion, chiles, ginger, and star anise and stir-fry for 1 minute. Add the bell pepper strips, zucchini, and baby corn and stir-fry for an additional 2 minutes.

4 Pour in the orange juice and soy sauce and continue to stir-fry for an additional 1 minute before adding the reserved shredded bok choy. Stir-fry for 2 minutes, or until the vegetables are tender but still firm to the bite. Arrange the warm salad on the bok choy-lined serving platter, scatter the cashew nuts over the top, and serve as 4 portions.

Mixed Cabbage Coleslaw

INGREDIENTS

serves 4
calories per
portion

96

3 oz/85 g red cabbage

3 oz/85 g hard white cabbage

2 oz/55 g green cabbage

2 carrots, about 6 oz/175 g,
peeled and grated

1 white onion, finely sliced

2 red apples, cored and
chopped

4 tbsp orange juice

2 celery stalks, trimmed and
finely sliced

2 oz/55 g canned corn kernels

2 tbsp raisins

FOR THE DRESSING

4 tbsp lowfat plain yogurt

1 tbsp chopped fresh parsley

pepper

1 Discard the outer leaves and hard central
core from the cabbages and shred finely.
Wash well in plenty of cold water and drain
thoroughly.

2 Place the cabbages in a bowl and stir in
the carrots and onion. Toss the apples in the
orange juice and add to the cabbages together
with any remaining orange juice, and the
celery, corn, and raisins. Mix well.

3 For the dressing, mix the yogurt, parsley, and
pepper to taste, in a bowl then pour over the
cabbage mixture. Stir and serve as 4 portions.

Fish & Mango Kabobs

INGREDIENTS

serves 4
calories per
kabob

96

3 oz/85 g fresh tuna steak

3 oz/85 g swordfish

1 zucchini, cut into chunks

1 fresh ripe mango, peeled
and cut into cubes (about
4 oz/115 g peeled flesh)

2 limes, cut into wedges

2 tbsp sweet chili sauce

4 tbsp lowfat plain yogurt

1 tbsp chopped fresh cilantro

FOR GARNISH
fresh herbs
lime wedges

1 Preheat the broiler to high and line the broiler rack with foil. Discard any bones from the fish and cut into bite-size pieces.

2 Thread the fish, zucchini, mango, and lime wedges onto 4 presoaked wooden skewers and brush lightly with 1 tablespoon of chili sauce.

3 Mix the yogurt, the remaining 1 tablespoon of chili sauce, and the chopped cilantro together in a bowl until smooth. Spoon into a serving dish, cover lightly, and chill in the refrigerator until required.

4 Cook the kabobs under the broiler for 5 to 7 minutes, or until the fish is cooked. Turn the kabobs at least once during cooking. Transfer to a serving plate, garnish with fresh herbs and lime wedges, and serve with the dipping sauce.

Chicken Sesame Kabobs

INGREDIENTS

serves 2
calories per
portion

94

4 oz/115 g skinless, boneless chicken breast, cut into thin strips, or chicken stir-fry strips

3 tbsp lemon juice

1½ tbsp soy sauce

1 tsp honey

6 oz/175 g assorted salad greens

1 red onion, thinly sliced

1 large carrot, peeled and grated

1 chicory head (optional)

bunch of radishes, trimmed, washed, and sliced

1 tbsp sesame seeds

3 tbsp lowfat plain yogurt

1 Thread the chicken onto 8 presoaked wooden skewers.

2 Mix 2 tablespoons of lemon juice, 1 tablespoon of soy sauce, and the honey together in a small bowl. Brush the mixture over the chicken and let marinate for at least 15 minutes.

3 Preheat the broiler to high and line the broiler rack with foil. Arrange the salad greens on a large serving platter and top with the sliced onion and grated carrot. Divide the chicory into separate leaves, if using, and place around the edge of the platter. Scatter over the radishes.

4 Cook the chicken kabobs under the broiler for 8 to 10 minutes or until the chicken is thoroughly cooked. Remove from the broiler and sprinkle with the sesame seeds.

5 Mix the yogurt, the remaining lemon juice, and soy sauce in a small bowl and drizzle over the salad. Serve 2 kabobs per portion.

Turkey & Plum Bites

INGREDIENTS

serves 4
calories per
portion

5 oz/140 g skinless turkey steaks, cut into bite-size pieces

4 pearl onions

2 ripe plums, pitted and cut into 4 wedges

2 tbsp plum sauce

2 tbsp orange juice

1 spray sunflower oil

1–2 fresh Thai chiles, seeded and sliced

1 small yellow bell pepper, seeded and cut into strips

4 oz/115 g bok choy, shredded

1 Thread the turkey onto 4 presoaked wooden skewers with the pearl onions and plum wedges.

2 Mix 1 tablespoon of plum sauce and 1 tablespoon of orange juice together in a small bowl and use to brush over the turkey kabobs. Let marinate for at least 15 minutes, longer if time permits.

3 Preheat the broiler to high and line the broiler rack with foil. Cook the kabobs under the broiler for 8 to 10 minutes, or until the turkey is thoroughly cooked. Turn the kabobs halfway through cooking.

4 Heat a wok until hot, spray with the oil, and heat for 30 seconds. Add the chiles and pepper strips and stir-fry for 1 to 2 minutes. Add the remaining plum sauce and orange juice and stir-fry for an additional 1 minute.

5 Stir in the bok choy, and stir-fry for 1 to 2 minutes, or until the vegetables are tender. Serve 1 kabob per person, with the vegetables.

Thai Crab Cakes

serves 6
calories per
portion

INGREDIENTS

10½ oz/300 g canned crabmeat, drained

1–2 fresh Thai chiles, seeded and finely chopped

6 scallions, trimmed and thinly sliced

5 oz/140 g zucchini, grated

4 oz/115 g carrot, peeled and grated

1 tbsp chopped fresh cilantro

2 tbsp cornstarch

2 egg whites

1 spray sunflower oil

FOR THE DIPPING SAUCE

⅔ cup lowfat plain yogurt

Tabasco sauce, to taste

2 tsp sesame seeds

lime wedges, to garnish

1 Place the crabmeat in a bowl and stir in the chiles, scallions, grated zucchini, and carrot with the chopped cilantro. Add the cornstarch and mix well.

2 Beat the egg whites together in a separate bowl then stir into the crab mixture and mix together.

3 Lightly spray a nonstick skillet with the oil then drop small spoonfuls of the crab mixture into the skillet. Pan-fry the crab cakes over low heat for 3 to 4 minutes, pressing down with the back of a spatula. Turn over halfway through cooking. Cook the crab cakes in batches.

4 Mix the yogurt and Tabasco sauce, to taste, in a small bowl and stir in the sesame seeds. Spoon into a small bowl and use as a dipping sauce with the cooked crab cakes. Serve garnished with lime wedges, divided among 6 plates, to be sure of even-size portions.

Potato, Leek & Feta Patties

INGREDIENTS

serves 4
calories per
portion

91

not including
tomato ketchup

1 whole garlic bulb

4 oz/115 g sweet potatoes,
peeled and cut into chunks

6 oz/175 g carrots, peeled
and chopped

4 oz/115 g leeks, trimmed
and finely chopped

2 oz/55 g feta cheese,
crumbled

1–2 tsp Tabasco sauce,
or to taste

1 tbsp chopped fresh cilantro

pepper

fresh herbs or salad, to
garnish

tomato ketchup, to serve
(optional)

1 Break the garlic bulb open, place in a small roasting pan, and roast for 20 minutes, or until soft. Remove and when cool enough to handle, squeeze out the roasted garlic flesh.

2 Cook the sweet potatoes and carrots in a large pan of boiling water for 15 minutes, or until soft. Drain and mash then mix in the roasted garlic flesh.

3 Add the leeks, feta cheese, Tabasco sauce to taste, cilantro, and pepper to the sweet potato mixture. Cover and let chill in the refrigerator for at least 30 minutes.

4 Preheat the oven to 375°F/190°C. Using slightly dampened hands, shape the sweet potato mixture into 8 small round patties and place on a nonstick baking sheet. Bake for 15 to 20 minutes, or until piping hot. Garnish with fresh herbs or salad and serve with tomato ketchup, if using. Divide the patties among 4 plates, 2 patties per person, to be sure of the portions.

Stuffed Peppers

INGREDIENTS

serves 4
calories per
pepper

95

4 assorted colored bell
peppers

6 scallions, trimmed and finely
chopped

4 oz/115 g pearl mushrooms,
chopped

2 tbsp sundried tomatoes,
chopped

1 tbsp chopped fresh mint

3 oz/85 g cooked or canned
fava beans, coarsely chopped

scant ¼ cup plumped dried
apricots, chopped

½ oz/15 g Parmesan cheese,
finely grated

pepper

salad greens, to serve
(optional)

1 Preheat the oven to 375°F/190°C. Cut the peppers in half and discard the seeds. Place the pepper halves in a large heatproof dish and cover with boiling water. Let stand for 10 minutes then drain and set aside.

2 Put the scallions, mushrooms, tomatoes, mint, fava beans, apricots, and pepper to taste in a large bowl and stir well. Use to fill the halved peppers, and place in a large ovenproof dish. Sprinkle cheese over the top of each filled pepper. Pour in about 2 inches/5 cm of hot water, cover loosely with foil, and cook in the oven for 25 minutes, or until the peppers are piping hot.

3 Remove and drain the peppers. Serve hot, either by themselves or with a salad.

Stuffed Zucchini

INGREDIENTS

serves 4
calories per
zucchini

4 zucchini, about 6 oz/175 g
each

1 spray olive oil

1 small onion, coarsely
chopped

2 garlic cloves, chopped

4 oz/115 g carrots, peeled and
grated

4 oz/115 g canned red kidney
beans, drained and rinsed

1 tbsp tomato paste (optional)

1 tbsp chopped fresh cilantro

⅔ cup water

4 tomatoes, thickly sliced

pepper

1 Preheat the oven to 375°F/190°C. Cut the zucchini in half lengthwise and scoop out the centers with a spoon. Chop the scooped out flesh and place in a food processor. Put the zucchini hollows into a large heatproof dish and pour over enough boiling water to cover. Let stand for 10 minutes then drain and set aside.

2 Add the oil, onion, garlic, carrot, beans, tomato paste, if using, and chopped cilantro to the food processor and process until blended. Use to stuff the hollowed-out zucchini and level the surface.

3 Place the filled zucchini in a large ovenproof dish and pour around the water. Cover loosely with foil and bake for 35 minutes.

4 Remove from the oven and place the sliced tomatoes on top. Return to the oven and continue to cook for an additional 10 minutes, or until the zucchini are tender and the filling is piping hot. Serve hot, sprinkled with the pepper.

Tomato Ratatouille

INGREDIENTS

serves 4
calories per
portion

92

4 sprays olive oil

1 onion, cut into small wedges

2–4 garlic cloves, chopped

1 small eggplant, trimmed and chopped

1 small red bell pepper, seeded and chopped

1 small yellow bell pepper, seeded and chopped

1 zucchini, trimmed and chopped

2 tbsp tomato paste

3 tbsp water

4 oz/115 g mushrooms, sliced if large

8 oz/225 g ripe tomatoes, chopped

pepper

1 tbsp shredded fresh basil, to garnish

1 oz/25 g Parmesan cheese, freshly shaved, to serve

1 Heat the oil in a heavy-bottom pan, add the onion, garlic, and eggplant and cook, stirring frequently for 3 minutes.

2 Add the peppers and zucchini. Mix the tomato paste and water together in a small bowl and stir into the pan. Bring to a boil, cover with a lid, reduce the heat to a simmer, and cook for 10 minutes.

3 Add the mushrooms and chopped tomatoes with pepper to taste and continue to simmer for 12 to 15 minutes, stirring occasionally, until the vegetables are tender.

4 Divide the ratatouille among 4 warmed bowls, garnish each with shredded basil, and serve with freshly shaved Parmesan cheese to sprinkle over.

Thai-Style Tom Yam

INGREDIENTS

serves 4
calories per
portion

97

7 oz/200 g raw shrimp, peeled and deveined, heads and tails removed and set aside

1.8 quarts water

2 lemongrass stalks, bruised

3 fresh Thai chiles, sliced

about ½-inch/1-cm piece fresh ginger, peeled and coarsely chopped

few fresh cilantro sprigs

1 large carrot, peeled and grated

3 oz/85 g green string beans, trimmed and chopped

1 oz/25 g thread egg noodles

1–2 tbsp Thai fish sauce

2 tbsp lime juice

4 oz/115 g fresh or canned straw mushrooms, trimmed or drained

pepper

few fresh cilantro leaves, to garnish

1 Put the reserved shrimp trimmings into a large pan, add the water, lemongrass stalks, 2 of the chiles, the fresh ginger, and a few cilantro sprigs and bring to a boil. Reduce the heat and simmer for 30 minutes then strain, discarding the solids and reserving the fish stock.

2 Pour the fish stock into a clean pan and add the remaining sliced chile with the carrot, beans, and egg noodles. Bring to a boil, then reduce the heat and simmer for 5 minutes.

3 Add the fish sauce, lime juice, and mushrooms together with the raw peeled shrimp and cook for 3 minutes, or until the shrimp are cooked and have turned pink. Add pepper if necessary, garnish with cilantro leaves, and serve, divided equally among 4 warmed bowls.

Warm Duck Salad

INGREDIENTS

serves 4
calories per
portion

98

6 oz/175 g duck breast,
all fat removed

2–3 sprays sunflower oil

1-inch/2.5-cm piece fresh
ginger, peeled and grated

1 fresh serrano chile, seeded
and sliced

1 red onion, cut into thin
wedges

2 celery stalks, trimmed and
finely sliced

1 small red bell pepper, seeded
and finely sliced

1 tbsp soy sauce

4 oz/115 g zucchini, trimmed
and sliced

2 ripe but still firm plums,
pitted and sliced

3 oz/85 g bok choy, shredded

1 tbsp chopped fresh cilantro

1 Cut the duck breast into thin strips and set
aside. Heat a wok until very hot then spray with
the oil and heat for 30 seconds. Add the ginger,
chile, and duck strips and stir-fry for 1 to
2 minutes, or until the duck strips are browned.

2 Add the onion wedges, celery, and pepper
slices and continue to stir-fry for 3 minutes.

3 Add the soy sauce, zucchini, and plums
to the wok and stir-fry for 2 minutes before
stirring in the shredded bok choy and the
chopped cilantro. Stir-fry for an additional
minute then serve, divided equally among
4 bowls.

3 Dinners

There are meat, fish, poultry, and vegetarian ideas contained in this chapter, all of which will enable you to watch your intake of calories while, at the same time, not miss out on any flavor. Choose from Gingered Shrimp Wraps, which are great for sharing, Beef, Pepper, and Mushroom Sauté, or a delicious Vegetable & Filo Pie, all of which are full of taste and crammed with health-giving nutrients.

Gingered Shrimp Wraps

serves 4
calories per portion

99

INGREDIENTS

5 oz/140 g carrots, peeled

3 celery stalks, trimmed

½ cucumber, peeled if preferred

1 red bell pepper, seeded

large lettuce leaves, such as iceberg

1–2 sprays sunflower oil

2–4 garlic cloves, crushed

1–2 fresh red jalapeño chiles, seeded and chopped

1-inch/2.5-cm piece fresh ginger, peeled and grated

2 tsp finely grated lime rind

3 tbsp lime juice

8 oz/225 g raw king shrimp, peeled and deveined

pepper

1 Cut the carrots, celery, cucumber, and red bell pepper into thin sticks. Place all the prepared vegetables and the lettuce leaves on a large serving platter and set aside.

2 Spray a nonstick skillet with the oil, add the garlic, chiles, and ginger and sauté for 1 minute, stirring continuously. Add the lime rind and juice and stir until well mixed.

3 Add the shrimp and cook, stirring, for 3 to 4 minutes, or until the shrimp have turned pink. Add pepper to taste then drain and place on the serving platter, to be served as 4 portions.

4 To eat, take a lettuce leaf, top with some prepared vegetables then some shrimp, fold over, and enjoy.

Curry-Topped Salmon

INGREDIENTS

serves 4
calories per
fillet

97

4 salmon fillets, about
6 oz/175 g each

scant 1 cup fresh whole wheat
breadcrumbs

1½ tbsp curry paste

1 tbsp chopped fresh cilantro

FOR GARNISH
lemon wedges
salad greens (optional)

1 Preheat the oven to 350°F/180°C. Discard any fine bones from the salmon fillets and rinse lightly. Pat dry with paper towels.

2 Mix the breadcrumbs, curry paste, and chopped cilantro together in a bowl until well blended.

3 Place each salmon fillet on a sheet of foil and pat the curry-flavored breadcrumbs on top of each. Cover with another sheet of foil and place on one or two large baking sheets.

4 Bake for 10 minutes then remove the top sheet of foil and cook for an additional 10 minutes, or until the salmon is tender. Serve garnished with lemon wedges and salad greens.

Sole with Oranges

INGREDIENTS

serves 4
calories per
fillet

99

4 sole fillets, about 4 oz/115 g each

1-inch/2.5-cm piece fresh ginger, peeled and grated

2–3 garlic cloves, crushed

1 tbsp grated orange rind

4 tbsp orange juice

1 tbsp soy sauce

salad, to serve

FOR GARNISH
orange wedges
fresh parsley

1 Remove any fine bones from the sole fillets and rinse lightly. Pat dry with paper towels and place in a large shallow dish.

2 Mix the ginger, garlic, orange rind and juice, and soy sauce together in a bowl and pour over the fish. Cover loosely and let marinate in the refrigerator for at least 30 minutes, longer if time permits. Spoon the marinade over the fish occasionally if marinating for longer.

3 Preheat the broiler to high and line the broiler rack with foil. Drain the fish from the marinade, reserving the marinade, and place the fish on the broiler rack. Broil for 4 to 5 minutes, or until cooked. Spoon a little of the marinade over the fish while cooking.

4 Remove the fish from the broiler rack, transfer to serving plates, garnish with orange wedges and parsley, and serve with salad.

Salsa Sole

INGREDIENTS

serves 4
calories per
fillet

87

4 sole fillets, about 3 oz/85 g each, skinned

3 tomatoes, peeled, seeded, and finely chopped

1 fresh jalapeño chile, seeded and finely chopped

4 scallions, trimmed and finely chopped

2-inch/5-cm piece cucumber, peeled and finely chopped

1 tbsp chopped fresh tarragon

⅓ cup cottage cheese

2 tbsp finely grated orange rind

4 tbsp water

pepper

orange wedges, to garnish

salad, to serve

1 Preheat the oven to 350°F/180°C. Lightly rinse the sole fillets, pat dry on paper towels, and set aside.

2 Put the tomatoes, chile, scallions, and cucumber in a bowl and stir in the tarragon. Beat in the cottage cheese and 1 tablespoon of the orange rind and add pepper to taste.

3 Place the sole fillets skinned-side down on the counter and spread the fillets with a little of the prepared salsa. Roll up each fillet and secure with a wooden toothpick or small skewer. Place in an ovenproof dish. Set aside the remaining salsa.

4 Blend the remaining orange rind with the water and pour around the fish. Cover with foil and cook for 15 to 20 minutes, or until the fish is cooked.

5 Remove the fish with a slotted spoon and place on individual serving plates. Garnish with orange wedges and serve with salad and the reserved salsa.

Sweet Potato & Tuna Fishcakes

INGREDIENTS

serves 4
calories per
fishcake

99

not including
green beans

6 oz/175 g sweet potatoes, peeled and chopped

6 oz/175 g canned tuna, in brine, drained

4 scallions, trimmed and chopped

1 tbsp grated lemon rind

1 tbsp chopped fresh cilantro

pepper

lemon wedges, to garnish

salad or freshly cooked green beans, to serve

1 Cook the sweet potatoes in a pan of boiling water for 10 to 12 minutes, or until tender when pierced with a fork. Drain and mash.

2 Flake the tuna then add to the mashed potatoes together with the chopped scallions, lemon rind, chopped cilantro, and pepper to taste.

3 Mix the ingredients lightly together then, using slightly dampened hands, shape into 4 circles. Place on a plate, cover loosely, and let chill in the refrigerator for at least 30 minutes, longer if time permits.

4 Preheat the oven to 375°F/190°C. Place the fishcakes on a large nonstick baking sheet and cook for 20 minutes, or until piping hot. Transfer to serving plates, garnish with lemon wedges, and serve with salad or freshly cooked green beans.

Seafood Stir-Fry

INGREDIENTS

serves 4
calories per
portion

4 oz/115 g white fish, such as monkfish fillet

2 sprays sunflower oil

1 fresh jalapeño chile, seeded and finely chopped

1-inch/2.5-cm piece fresh ginger, peeled and grated

3 oz/85 g raw shrimp, peeled and deveined

4 oz/115 g baby corn, sliced in half lengthwise

4 oz/115 g snow peas, trimmed

6 scallions, trimmed and chopped

1 tbsp soy sauce

4 oz/115 g squid, cleaned and cut into thin slices

4 oz/115 g fresh spinach leaves

¾ cup bean sprouts

1 Discard any skin from the white fish, rinse lightly, and pat dry on paper towels. Cut into small pieces.

2 Heat a wok and when hot, add the oil and heat for 10 seconds. Add the chile and ginger and stir-fry for 1 minute then add the white fish and shrimp and stir-fry for 2 minutes.

3 Add the baby corn, snow peas, scallions, and soy sauce and continue to stir-fry for 2 to 3 minutes, or until the fish is just cooked and the shrimp have almost turned completely pink.

4 Add the squid, spinach, and bean sprouts and continue to stir-fry for an additional 2 minutes, or until the fish, shrimp, and squid are cooked. Serve immediately, divided equally among 4 warmed bowls.

Seared Scallops

INGREDIENTS

serves 4
calories per
portion

10½ oz/300 g fresh scallops

1 tsp sunflower oil

2-inch/5-cm piece fresh ginger,
peeled and grated

1 tbsp finely grated lime rind

1 orange bell pepper, seeded
and sliced

1 red onion, thinly sliced

4 oz/115 g wild mushrooms,
such as chanterelle, or cremini
mushrooms

¼ cup lime juice

1 tsp honey (optional)

1 tbsp soy sauce

4 oz/115 g bok choy, shredded

1 Lightly rinse the scallops, discarding any thin black veins. Pat dry with paper towels and set aside.

2 Heat a wok and when hot add the oil. Add the grated ginger and cook, stirring for 1 minute.

3 Add the lime rind, bell pepper slices, and onion and stir-fry for 3 to 4 minutes, or until the onion has softened.

4 Add the scallops and mushrooms to the wok and stir-fry for 2 minutes. Make sure that the scallops are turned over after 1 minute.

5 Pour in the lime juice, add the honey, if using, and the soy sauce. Stir together, then add the bok choy and continue to cook for 2 to 3 minutes, or until the scallops are tender. Serve immediately, divided equally among 4 warmed bowls.

Vegetable & Filo Pie

serves 4
calories per
portion

INGREDIENTS

6 oz/175 g carrots, peeled and chopped

5 oz/140 g broccoli, divided into small florets

4 oz/115 g fava beans

scant 1/2 cup frozen or canned corn kernels

1¼ cups vegetable stock

1 tbsp cornstarch

2 tbsp water

1 tbsp chopped fresh cilantro

3 sheets filo dough

pepper

1 Preheat the oven to 375°F/190°C. Cook the carrots in a pan of boiling water for 6 minutes, then add the broccoli florets with the fava beans and cook for an additional 2 minutes. Stir in the corn, mix then drain thoroughly and set aside.

2 Heat the stock in another pan, add the vegetables, and bring to boiling point. Blend the cornstarch with the water in a bowl and stir the paste into the boiling liquid. Cook, stirring, until the sauce thickens. Stir in the chopped cilantro and add pepper to taste. Spoon the mixture into a 5-cup/1.2-liter pie dish and let cool.

3 Place the filo dough on the counter and brush one sheet lightly with a little water. Put a second sheet on top. Place the filo dough over the filling, pressing the edges over the filling to encase completely.

4 Brush the top of the pie with a little water and put the remaining sheet of dough decoratively on top. Bake for 25 minutes, or until the top is golden brown. Serve a quarter of the pie per person.

Turkey & Eggplant Curry

INGREDIENTS

serves 4
calories per
portion

2 sprays sunflower oil

1 onion, chopped

2 garlic cloves, crushed

1–2 fresh serrano chiles,
seeded and chopped

1 tsp ground cumin

1 tsp ground coriander

½ tsp turmeric

1 small eggplant, about
8 oz/225 g, trimmed and cut
into small cubes

8 oz/225 g skinless, boneless
turkey breast, cut into cubes

2 carrots, about 6 oz/175 g,
peeled and chopped

1 small red bell pepper, seeded
and chopped

2 cups chicken stock

1 tbsp chopped fresh cilantro,
to garnish

1 Heat a large nonstick pan and add the oil.
Add the onion, garlic, and chiles and cook,
stirring, for 2 minutes. Sprinkle in all of the
spices and cook, stirring continuously, for an
additional 2 minutes.

2 Add the eggplant and turkey cubes and cook,
stirring, for 5 minutes, or until the turkey is
browned all over. Add the carrots and red
pepper, stir, then pour in the stock. Bring to
a boil, cover with a lid, and simmer for 20 to
25 minutes, or until the turkey is tender.

3 Sprinkle with chopped cilantro and serve,
divided equally among 4 warmed bowls.

The Perfect Burger

serves 4
calories per
burger

INGREDIENTS

6 oz/175 g fresh lean beef, such as round, ground

2 shallots, finely chopped

1 tbsp Worcestershire sauce, or to taste

pepper

2 sprays sunflower oil

2 onions, thinly sliced

4 beef tomatoes

1–2 garlic cloves, peeled

tomato ketchup, to serve (optional)

1 Put the ground beef in a bowl and add the shallots, Worcestershire sauce, and pepper to taste. Mix together then, with damp hands, shape into 4 equal-size burgers. Place the burgers on a plate, cover lightly with plastic wrap, and chill until required.

2 Preheat the broiler to high and line the broiler rack with foil. Heat a nonstick skillet, spray with the oil, and add the sliced onion. Cook over low heat for 12 to 15 minutes, stirring frequently until the onions are tender. Keep warm if necessary.

3 Cut the tomatoes into thick slices and the garlic cloves into slivers. Stud the tomatoes with the garlic and place on the broiler rack together with the burgers.

4 Cook the burgers for 3 to 4 minutes on each side, or according to personal preference. If the tomatoes are cooking too quickly, either remove them and add a little later or remove and keep warm.

5 Serve each burger between the thick tomato slices with the onion garnish and ketchup, if using.

Seared Duck with Red Onion Relish

INGREDIENTS

serves 4
calories per
duck breast

98

7 oz/200 g duck breast (after all fat and skin is removed)

1 tbsp orange rind

1⅓ cups water, plus 1 extra tbsp

2 tbsp balsamic vinegar or red wine vinegar

2 sprays sunflower oil

2 red onions, very thinly sliced

2 garlic cloves, crushed

1 tsp dark brown sugar

1 tsp cornstarch

bitter salad greens, to serve

FOR GARNISH
1 tbsp chopped fresh parsley
orange wedges

1 Lightly rinse the duck breast, pat dry with paper towels, slice thinly, and put in a nonmetallic dish that will not react with acid.

2 Blend the orange rind with ⅔ cup water and 1 tablespoon of vinegar in a bowl and pour over the duck. Cover lightly with plastic wrap, and let marinate for at least 20 minutes. Stir occasionally during marinating.

3 Meanwhile, heat a nonstick pan and spray with the oil. Add the onion and garlic and cook, stirring, over low heat for 5 minutes. Sprinkle in the sugar, then add the remaining water and vinegar. Cover and cook for 10 minutes, or until the onions are soft. Keep warm.

4 Heat a nonstick heavy-bottom skillet, add the duck breasts with the marinade, and cook gently for 6 minutes. Add the cooked onions with any liquor and stir together lightly.

5 Blend the cornstarch with 1 tablespoon of water and stir into the skillet. Cook, stirring, until the liquid has thickened, then cook for an additional 2 minutes, or until the duck is tender and the onions are hot. Garnish with parsley and orange wedges, and serve immediately, with salad.

Vegetable Chili

INGREDIENTS

serves 4
calories per
portion

97

not including
pumpkin mash

2–3 sprays olive oil

1 onion, chopped

1–2 fresh serrano chiles,
seeded and chopped

2–3 garlic cloves, chopped

2 celery stalks, trimmed
and sliced

6 oz/175 g carrots, peeled
and chopped

7 oz/200 g canned chopped
tomatoes

2/3 cup water

1 tbsp tomato paste

4 oz/115 g canned red kidney
beans, drained and rinsed

4 oz/115 g green beans,
trimmed and chopped

pepper

1 tbsp chopped fresh cilantro

freshly cooked mashed
pumpkin, to serve (optional)

1 Heat a large pan, spray with the oil, and add
the onion, chiles, and garlic. Cook over low
heat, stirring continuously for 5 minutes. Add
the celery, carrots, and chopped tomatoes.
Pour the water into the empty tomato can,
swirl around, then pour it into the pan. Add the
tomato paste and bring to a boil.

2 Reduce the heat to a gentle simmer then
cover with a lid and simmer for 10 minutes.
Add the red kidney beans together with the
green beans and continue to simmer for an
additional 10 minutes, or until the vegetables
are tender.

3 Season with pepper to taste and add the
chopped cilantro. Serve, divided equally among
4 warmed bowls, with pumpkin mash, if using.

Roasted Vegetables

INGREDIENTS

serves 4
calories per
portion

1 onion, cut into wedges

2–4 garlic cloves, left whole
but peeled

1 eggplant, about 8 oz/225 g,
trimmed and cut into cubes

2 zucchini, about 6 oz/175 g,
trimmed and cut into chunks

10½ oz/300 g butternut squash,
peeled, seeded, and cut into
small wedges

2 assorted colored bell
peppers, seeded and cut into
chunks

2 tsp olive oil

pepper

1 tbsp shredded fresh basil

1 Preheat the oven to 400°F/200°C. Place the onion wedges, whole garlic, and eggplant cubes in a large roasting pan.

2 Add the zucchini, squash, and peppers to the roasting pan then pour over the oil. Turn the vegetables until they are lightly coated in the oil.

3 Roast the vegetables for 35 to 40 minutes, or until softened but not mushy. Turn the vegetables over occasionally during cooking.

4 Remove the vegetables from the oven, season with pepper to taste, and stir. Scatter with shredded basil and serve divided among 4 warmed bowls while still warm.

Roasted Butternut Squash

INGREDIENTS

serves 4
calories per
portion

1 butternut squash, about
1 lb/450 g

1 onion, chopped

2–3 garlic cloves, crushed

4 small tomatoes, chopped

3 oz/85 g cremini mushrooms,
chopped

3 oz/85 g canned lima beans,
drained, rinsed, and coarsely
chopped

1 zucchini, about 4 oz/115 g,
trimmed and grated

1 tbsp chopped fresh oregano,
plus extra to garnish

pepper

2 tbsp tomato paste

1¼ cups water

4 scallions, trimmed and
chopped

1 tbsp Worcestershire or Hot
Pepper sauce, or to taste

1 Preheat the oven to 375°F/190°C. Prick the squash all over with a metal skewer then roast for 40 minutes, or until tender. Remove from the oven and leave until cool enough to handle.

2 Cut the squash in half, scoop out and discard the seeds then scoop out some of the flesh, making hollows in both halves. Chop the cooked flesh and put in a bowl. Place the two halves side by side in a large roasting pan.

3 Add the onion, garlic, chopped tomatoes, and mushrooms to the cooked squash flesh. Add the coarsely chopped lima beans, grated zucchini, chopped oregano, and pepper to taste and mix well. Spoon the filling into the 2 halves of the squash, packing it down as firmly as possible.

4 Mix the tomato paste with the water, scallions, and Worcestershire sauce in a small bowl and pour around the squash.

5 Cover loosely with a large sheet of foil and bake for 30 minutes, or until piping hot. Serve, divided equally among 4 warmed bowls, garnished with extra chopped oregano.

Beef, Pepper & Mushroom Sauté

serves 4
calories per
portion

99

INGREDIENTS

2 sprays olive oil

6 oz/175 g beef steak, such as round (fat or gristle removed), cut into thin strips

2 shallots, cut into small wedges

1–2 garlic cloves, chopped

2 assorted colored bell peppers, seeded and cut into thin strips

6 oz/175 g large portobello mushrooms, sliced

⅔ cup beef stock

1–2 tsp red currant preserve (optional)

1 tbsp chopped fresh parsley

1 Heat a nonstick skillet, spray with oil, and heat for 30 seconds. Add the steak strips and stir-fry for 1 minute, or until browned. Remove from the skillet and set aside.

2 Add the shallots, garlic, and peppers to the skillet and cook, stirring, for 2 minutes. Add the mushrooms, stir well, pour in the stock, and add the red currant preserve, if using. Bring to a boil, reduce the heat to a simmer, and cook for 4 minutes.

3 Return the beef steak strips to the skillet and cook for an additional 2 to 4 minutes, or until the steak and vegetables are cooked to your taste. Sprinkle with the parsley and serve, divided equally among 4 warmed bowls.

Turkey & Apricot Tagine

INGREDIENTS

serves 4
calories per
portion

98

2 sprays olive oil

8 oz/225 g turkey breast steaks,
cut into bite-size pieces

1 onion, chopped

2–3 garlic cloves, chopped

1 small eggplant, about
8 oz/225 g

1 tsp ground cinnamon

1 tsp ground cumin

1 tsp ground coriander

few saffron strands

2 cups chicken stock

⅓ cup plumped dried apricots,
chopped

pepper

1 tbsp chopped fresh cilantro

1 Heat a nonstick pan and spray with the oil.
Then add the turkey pieces and cook for 2 to
3 minutes, or until browned. Remove from the
pan with a slotted spoon and set aside.

2 Add the onion, garlic, and eggplant to the
pan and cook, stirring, for 5 minutes, or until
the onion is beginning to soften. Sprinkle in all
the spices including the saffron and cook,
stirring, for 3 minutes. Pour in the stock, bring
to a boil then reduce the heat to a simmer.

3 Return the turkey to the pan. Cover with a lid
and cook for 15 minutes. Add the dried apricots
to the pan and season with pepper to taste.
Continue to simmer for 10 minutes, or until
the turkey is tender. Sprinkle with chopped
cilantro and serve, divided equally among
4 warmed bowls.

Barbecued Chicken

INGREDIENTS

serves 4
calories per
drumstick

99

4 chicken drumsticks, about
3½ oz/100 g each, skinned

1 tbsp chopped fresh parsley

lemon wedges

salad, to serve

FOR THE SAUCE

1 shallot, finely chopped

1 garlic clove, crushed

1 tbsp tomato paste blended
with ⅔ cup water

2 tbsp red wine vinegar

1 tbsp prepared mustard

1 tbsp Worcestershire sauce

1 To make the sauce, place the shallot, garlic, tomato paste mixture, red wine vinegar, mustard, and Worcestershire sauce in a screw-top jar, cover with the lid, and shake vigorously until well blended.

2 Rinse the chicken drumsticks and pat dry with paper towels. Place the drumsticks in a large ovenproof dish, pour over the sauce, and let stand for at least 2 hours, occasionally spooning the sauce over the chicken.

3 Preheat the oven to 375°F/190°C. Cook the chicken drumsticks in the oven for 20 to 25 minutes, or until thoroughly cooked. Spoon the sauce over the chicken or turn the chicken over during cooking.

4 Transfer to a serving plate, sprinkle with chopped parsley, garnish with lemon wedges, and serve with salad.

Mushroom-Stuffed Turkey

INGREDIENTS

serves 4
calories per
scallop

98

4 turkey scallops, about
3 oz/85 g each

4 scallions, trimmed and finely
chopped

1–2 garlic cloves, chopped

3 oz/85 g pearl mushrooms

1 tomato, seeded

pepper

fresh basil sprigs or salad
greens, to garnish

1 Preheat the oven to 375°F/190°C. Place the turkey scallops between two sheets of parchment paper and pound lightly with a meat mallet or rolling pin until about ¼ inch/ 5 mm thick. Take care not to tear the flesh. Keep covered and set aside.

2 Place the scallions, garlic, mushrooms, tomato, and pepper to taste in a food processor and process for 1 minute, or until finely chopped.

3 Divide the stuffing into 4 portions and use to spread over the turkey scallops. Roll up the scallops to encase the stuffing and secure with either string or wooden toothpicks. Cut out four 6-inch/15-cm squares of parchment paper and wrap each turkey scallop in a square of paper.

4 Place the parcels in a roasting pan and bake for 20 to 25 minutes, or until the turkey is thoroughly cooked. Remove and serve sliced with a garnish of basil sprigs or salad greens.

Chinese Lemon Chicken

serves 4
calories per
portion

96

INGREDIENTS

10½ oz/300 g skinless,
boneless chicken breast

chopped fresh herbs,
to garnish

FOR THE MARINADE

⅔ cup freshly squeezed lemon
juice

1 tbsp light soy sauce

1 tbsp cornstarch

1 Lightly rinse the chicken and pat dry with paper towels. Cut into bite-size cubes and place in a shallow dish.

2 Mix the lemon juice and soy sauce together in a bowl. Put the cornstarch in another bowl and stir in the lemon and soy mixture to form a paste. Spread over the chicken and let marinate for 15 minutes.

3 Heat a nonstick skillet and add the chicken and marinade. Cook, stirring, for 10 to 12 minutes, or until the chicken is thoroughly cooked. Transfer to 4 serving plates, pour over the sauce, and serve, garnished with fresh herbs.

Beef Stir-Fry

INGREDIENTS

serves 4
calories per portion

2–3 sprays olive oil

5 oz/140 g beef steak, such as round (fat removed), cut into thin strips

1 orange bell pepper, seeded and cut into thin strips

4 scallions, trimmed and chopped

1–2 fresh jalapeño chiles, seeded and chopped

2–3 garlic cloves, chopped

4 oz/115 g snow peas, trimmed and cut in half diagonally

4 oz/115 g large portobello mushrooms, sliced

1–2 tsp hoisin sauce, or to taste

1 tbsp orange juice

3 oz/85 g arugula or watercress sprigs

1 Heat a wok then spray in the oil and heat for 30 seconds. Add the beef and stir-fry for 1 minute or until browned. Using a slotted spoon, remove and set aside.

2 Add the pepper, scallions, chiles, and garlic and stir-fry for 2 minutes. Add the snow peas and mushrooms and stir-fry for an additional 2 minutes.

3 Return the beef to the wok and add the hoisin sauce and orange juice. Stir-fry for 2 to 3 minutes, or until the beef is tender and the vegetables are tender but still firm to the bite. Stir in the arugula and stir-fry until it starts to wilt. Serve immediately, divided equally among 4 warmed bowls.

4 Desserts

Watching your calorie intake does not necessarily mean missing out on the sweeter things of life. Fruit, which is one of the "superfoods" and essential for a healthy diet, provides the basis for most of the recipes featured in this chapter. Try the Fruity Stuffed Nectarines, a spoonful of Strawberry & Balsamic Vinegar Semifreddo to cool you down, or when you're feeling like spoiling yourself, a very thin slice of Chocolate Jelly Roll.

Fruity Stuffed Nectarines

INGREDIENTS

serves 4
calories per
nectarine

84

4 ripe but firm nectarines
or peaches

5 oz/140 g blueberries

4 oz/115 g fresh raspberries

⅔ cup freshly squeezed
orange juice

1–2 tsp honey, or to taste

1 tbsp brandy (optional)

scant 1 cup lowfat strained
plain yogurt

1 tbsp finely grated orange
rind

1 Preheat the oven to 350°F/180°C. Cut the nectarines in half and remove the pits then place in a shallow ovenproof dish.

2 Mix the blueberries and raspberries together in a bowl and use to fill the hollows left by the removal of the nectarine pits. Spoon any extra berries around the nectarines.

3 Mix together the orange juice, honey, and brandy, if using, in a small bowl and pour over the fruit. Blend the yogurt with the grated orange rind in another bowl and let chill in the refrigerator until required.

4 Bake the berry-filled nectarines for 10 minutes, or until the fruit is hot. Serve with the orange-flavored yogurt.

Aromatic Pears

INGREDIENTS

serves 4
calories per
pear

90

4 ripe but firm pears, about
5 oz/140 g each

2 tbsp lemon juice

1 tbsp honey, or to taste

1 fresh jalapeño chile, seeded

2 whole star anise

1 cinnamon stick, bruised

1 lemongrass stalk, bruised

½-inch/1-cm piece fresh
ginger, peeled and sliced

2 whole cloves

4 fresh bay leaves

1¼ cups water

1 Using a vegetable peeler, peel the pears as thinly as possible and leave the stalk intact. If necessary, cut off a thin slice from the base of each pear so it will stand upright. Place in a large bowl and pour over the lemon juice with enough water to cover the pears.

2 Pour the honey into a large pan with a lid. Add the chile, star anise, cinnamon stick, lemongrass stalk, ginger, cloves, bay leaves, and the water. Bring to a boil, then reduce the heat and simmer, stirring occasionally for 5 minutes, or until the honey has dissolved.

3 Drain the pears and place in the pan. Bring to almost boiling point then reduce the heat to a gentle simmer and cover with the lid.

4 Cook for 15 to 20 minutes, or until the pears are tender. Remove the pan from the heat and let the pears cool in the syrup. When cool, remove from the pan with a slotted spoon and place in a serving dish.

5 Return the syrup to the heat and bring to a boil. Boil for 5 to 8 minutes, or until reduced by half and the syrup has thickened. Let cool for 5 to 10 minutes then pour over the pears and serve.

Apricot Granita

INGREDIENTS

serves 4
calories per
glass

1 lb/450 g fresh apricots

1 tbsp honey, or to taste

1¼ cups water

2 ripe passion fruit, about
2 oz/55 g each or 2 whole
star anise and 5 bruised
cardamom pods

4 red currants, to decorate

2 raspberries, to decorate
(optional)

2 strawberries, halved, to
decorate (optional)

2 seedless grapes, halved, to
decorate (optional)

1 Set the freezer to rapid freeze at least 2 hours before making the granita. Cut the apricots in half, discard the pits, and set aside.

2 Pour the honey into a pan and add the water. Scoop out the seeds and juice from the passion fruit and add these, or the spices, to the pan. Bring to a boil then reduce the heat to a simmer and cook gently for 5 minutes.

3 Add the halved apricots to the pan, cover with a lid, and simmer for 10 to 12 minutes, or until tender. Remove from the heat and cool.

4 Drain the apricots (discard the spices if used), reserve the juice, then transfer the apricots to a food processor and process for 1 to 2 minutes to form a purée, slowly adding a little of the juice to slacken, if necessary.

5 Pour the purée into a freezerproof container and place in the freezer for 2 to 2½ hours, or until semi-frozen. Stir at least twice during the freezing time to break up the ice particles forming around the edges.

6 Once semi-frozen, serve spoonfuls in tall dessert glasses decorated with red currants, berries, and grapes, if using. Return the freezer to its original setting afterward.

Fruity Yogurt Cups

INGREDIENTS

serves 4
calories per
cup

2 cups lowfat plain yogurt

1½ tbsp finely grated orange rind

8 oz/225 g mixed berries, such as blueberries, raspberries, and strawberries, plus extra to decorate

fresh mint sprigs, to decorate (optional)

1 Set the freezer to rapid freeze at least 2 hours before freezing this dish. Line a 12-hole muffin pan with 12 paper cake cases, or use small ramekin dishes placed on a baking sheet.

2 Mix the yogurt and orange rind together in a large bowl. Cut any large strawberries into pieces so that they are the same size as the blueberries and raspberries.

3 Add the fruit to the yogurt then spoon into the paper cases or ramekins. Freeze for 2 hours, or until just frozen. Decorate with extra fruit and mint sprigs, if using, and serve. Remember to return the freezer to its original setting afterward.

Strawberry & Balsamic Vinegar Semifreddo

serves 4
calories per glass

65

INGREDIENTS

1 tsp honey

⅓ cup water

1 lb/450 g ripe strawberries, hulled

2 tbsp balsamic vinegar

4 baby strawberries or wild strawberries, halved, to decorate (optional)

fresh mint sprigs, to decorate (optional)

1 Set the freezer to rapid freeze at least 2 hours before freezing. Pour the honey and water into a pan and bring to a boil, stirring occasionally. Reduce the heat to a simmer then add the strawberries and simmer for 2 minutes. Remove from the heat and let cool.

2 Place the strawberries and syrup in a food processor with the balsamic vinegar and process for 30 seconds, or until a chunky mixture is formed.

3 Pour the mixture into a freezerproof container and freeze for 1 to 1½ hours, or until semifrozen. Stir at least once during freezing. Scoop spoonfuls of the semifreddo into glasses, and serve decorated with baby strawberries or wild strawberries, and mint sprigs, if using. Remember to return the freezer to its original setting afterward.

Apple & Mango Gelatin Dessert

INGREDIENTS

serves 8
calories per
portion

59

2 cups clear apple juice

1 tbsp honey

3 tsp powdered gelatin

1 large ripe mango, peeled and chopped into small pieces

10½ oz/300 g fresh blueberries or raspberries

1 Fill a 5-cup/1.2-liter mold or loaf pan with cold water and set aside. Pour the apple juice into a pan and add the honey. Place over low heat and sprinkle in the gelatin. Bring to a boil, whisking continuously, then remove and let cool for at least 5 minutes.

2 Drain the mold or loaf pan and place a layer of mango and blueberries in the base. Pour in enough of the cooled apple mixture to cover then leave in the refrigerator until set. Repeat the layers until all the fruits and apple mixture are used.

3 Let set in the refrigerator for 2 hours then cover the top with plastic wrap and weigh down with a few weights or clean cans. Let chill overnight.

4 The next day, dip the base into boiling water for about 30 seconds. Invert onto a serving platter and carefully remove the container. Serve, divided equally among 8 plates.

Ruby Fruits with Baby Meringues

serves 4
calories per
portion

98

INGREDIENTS

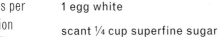

FOR THE MERINGUES

1 egg white

scant ¼ cup superfine sugar

FOR THE FRUIT

8 oz/225 g fresh or frozen
raspberries

2 tsp honey

scant 1 cup water

12 oz/350 g mixed fresh fruits,
such as raspberries,
strawberries, black currants,
and pitted cherries

few fresh mint sprigs, to
decorate

1 Preheat the oven to 250°F/120°C and line a baking sheet with parchment paper.

2 Whisk the egg white in a grease-free bowl until stiff then gradually add the sugar a spoonful at a time, whisking well after each addition. When all the sugar has been added and the mixture is stiff, spoon into a pastry bag fitted with a large star tip and pipe small whirls onto the lined baking sheet. Alternatively, shape the mounds with 2 teaspoons.

3 Bake in the oven for 1 hour, or until crisp. Let cool before removing from the baking sheet. Store in an airtight container.

4 Place the raspberries in a pan with the honey and water. Bring to a boil then reduce the heat to a simmer and cook for 5 to 8 minutes, or until the raspberries have collapsed. Let cool for 5 minutes. Transfer to a food processor and process to form a purée.

5 Press the purée through a strainer, adding a little extra water if the purée is too thick.

6 Prepare the fresh fruits and stir into the purée. Stir until coated and serve with the baby meringues and decorated with mint.

Stewed Creamy Apple

INGREDIENTS

serves 4
calories per
portion

1 lb/450 g cooking apples, peeled, cored, and chopped

1 tbsp honey, or to taste

1 tsp ground cinnamon

2–3 tbsp water

1¼ cups lowfat strained plain yogurt

5 oz/140 g fresh raspberries

few fresh mint sprigs, to decorate

1 Place the apples in a pan with the honey, cinnamon, and water then place over low heat. Cook, stirring occasionally, for 12 to 15 minutes, or until the apples are soft and fluffy. Remove from the heat and beat until free from any lumps. Let cool.

2 Place the yogurt in a large bowl and stir in the apples. Set aside a few fresh raspberries for decoration then stir the remainder gently into the apple mixture. Spoon into 4 individual dishes and chill for at least 1 hour.

3 Decorate with the reserved raspberries and the mint sprigs and serve.

Orange Cups

INGREDIENTS

serves 4
calories per
portion

98

4 large oranges

1 cup buttermilk
or lowfat plain yogurt

1 tsp honey

1 tsp chocolate shavings
(optional)

1 Set the freezer to rapid freeze at least 2 hours before freezing. To ensure that the oranges stand upright, cut a thin slice from the base of each. Cut a lid from each orange at the other end and set aside. Carefully cut down the inside of each orange and remove the pith and flesh from each. Do this over a bowl to catch all the juice.

2 Discard the pith from the scooped out flesh, then chop the flesh to make a chunky purée. Place in a bowl with the juice. Stir in the buttermilk and the honey, and pour into a freezerproof container. Freeze for 1 hour. Place the empty orange shells upside down on paper towels and let drain.

3 Remove the orange mixture from the freezer and stir well, breaking up any ice crystals. Return to the freezer for an additional 30 minutes, or until semi-frozen.

4 Stir again and use to fill the orange shells. Stand the filled oranges upright in a container. Freeze for an additional hour, or until frozen.

5 Before serving, transfer to the refrigerator for 30 minutes to soften slightly. Serve decorated with chocolate shavings, if using.

Summer Pavlova

INGREDIENTS

serves 6
calories per
portion

73

FOR THE MERINGUES

2 egg whites

scant ¼ cup superfine sugar

1 tsp cornstarch

1 tsp vanilla extract

1 tsp vinegar

FOR THE FILLING

1⅓ cups lowfat cream cheese

⅔ cup lowfat plain yogurt

½–1 tsp vanilla extract, or
to taste

10½ oz/300 g mixed berries

1 Preheat the oven to 250°F/120°C and line a baking sheet with nonstick parchment paper. Whisk the egg whites in a grease-free bowl until stiff then gradually add the sugar a spoonful at a time, whisking well after each addition. Stir in the cornstarch, vanilla extract, and the vinegar.

2 When all the sugar has been added and the mixture is stiff, spoon onto the lined baking sheet and form into a 6-inch/15-cm circle, hollowing out the center to form a case.

3 Bake in the oven for 1½ to 2 hours, or until crisp. Switch the oven off and let cool in the oven. Remove from the oven and leave until cold before removing from the baking sheet. Store in an airtight container until required.

4 Beat the cream cheese and yogurt together in a bowl until well blended, then stir in the vanilla extract. Clean the fruits if necessary, cutting any large fruits into bite-size pieces. When ready to serve, pile the cheese filling in the center of the pavlova case, top with the fruits, and serve cut into 6 slices.

Baked Apples

INGREDIENTS

serves 4
calories per
apple

4 cooking apples, about
8 oz/225 g each

3 oz/85 g blueberries

2 tbsp maple syrup, or to taste

6 tbsp water

lowfat strained plain yogurt,
to serve

1 Preheat the oven to 400°F/200°C. Using an apple corer or small, sharp-pointed knife, remove the central core. Make a thin slit around the center of each apple skin. If necessary, cut off a thin slice from the base of each apple to ensure that the apples stand upright. Place the apples in a large ovenproof dish.

2 Fill the center of each apple with the blueberries and pour the maple syrup over the apples. Add the water to the dish and bake for 45 minutes to 1 hour, or until the flesh feels tender when pierced lightly with a knife.

3 Remove from the oven and serve with lowfat strained plain yogurt.

Oat Buns

INGREDIENTS

makes 12
calories per
bun

2 cups rolled oats

heaping ¼ cup light brown
sugar

⅓ cup plumped dried apricots,
chopped

2 tbsp dried cranberries

2 tbsp slivered almonds

1 tsp ground cinnamon

2 egg whites

1 Preheat the oven to 375°F/190°C. Line a 12-hole muffin pan with 12 paper cases. Place the oats in a mixing bowl and add the sugar, apricots, cranberries, almonds, and cinnamon.

2 Beat the egg whites in another bowl until frothy, then stir into the dry ingredients and mix well together. Using your hands, take about 1 tablespoon of the mixture and press together. Place in a paper case. Continue until all the mixture has been used up.

3 Bake for 15 to 20 minutes, or until the tops are beginning to crisp. Remove from the oven and leave until cold before serving.

Chocolate Jelly Roll

INGREDIENTS

serves 12
calories per
slice

3 eggs

heaping ⅓ cup superfine
sugar, plus extra for sprinkling

1 tbsp unsweetened cocoa

scant 1 cup self-rising flour

1 tbsp boiled water, cooled

FOR THE FILLING

1 cup cottage cheese or lowfat
cream cheese

1 tbsp finely grated orange
rind

2 tsp honey

1 Preheat the oven to 425°F/220°C. Line a
12 x 9-inch/30 x 23-cm jelly roll pan with
nonstick parchment paper.

2 Break the eggs into a heatproof bowl and
add the sugar. Place the bowl over a pan of
simmering water and whisk until the whisk
leaves a trail when dragged across the surface.
Remove from the heat and whisk until cool.

3 Sift the cocoa and flour together in a
separate bowl, then stir lightly into the egg
mixture. Add the cooled boiled water, stir, then
pour into the prepared pan. Tap the pan lightly
on the counter to remove any air bubbles.

4 Bake for 8 to 10 minutes, or until the top
springs back lightly when touched. Remove
from the oven. Invert the cake onto parchment
paper, sprinkled with superfine sugar. Remove
the pan and carefully strip off the parchment
paper. Place a further sheet of paper on top
then carefully roll up and leave until cold.

5 To make the filling, beat the cheese, orange
rind, and honey together in a bowl. When the
jelly roll is cold unroll and spread with the
cottage cheese mixture, then carefully roll up.
Trim the edges and serve cut into thin slices.

Fresh Fruit Wedges

INGREDIENTS

serves 10
calories per
wedge

99

sunflower oil, for oiling

2 eggs

heaping ¼ cup superfine sugar

1 tbsp finely grated lemon rind

scant ½ cup self-rising flour,
sifted

1 tbsp freshly squeezed lemon
juice, strained

**FOR THE FILLING
AND DECORATION**

12 oz/350 g ripe plums or other
fruits of your choice

1 cup lowfat plain set yogurt

1 tsp confectioners' sugar,
sifted

1 Preheat the oven to 425°F/220°C. Lightly oil
and base line a 9-inch/23-cm cake pan with
nonstick parchment paper.

2 Break the eggs into a heatproof bowl and
add the superfine sugar and lemon rind. Place
the bowl over a pan of gently simmering water
and whisk until the whisk leaves a trail when it
is dragged lightly across the surface. Remove
from the heat and whisk until cool.

3 Add the flour to the bowl and stir very lightly
into the whisked mixture, taking care not to
overmix. Add the lemon juice and stir lightly
then pour into the prepared pan. Tap lightly on
the counter to remove any air bubbles.

4 Bake for 8 to 10 minutes, or until the top
springs back lightly when touched. Remove
from the oven and let cool for 10 minutes
before turning out, discarding the lining paper.

5 Halve the plums, discard the pits, and slice.

6 Place the sponge cake on a serving plate and
spoon the yogurt on top. Arrange the plums
over. Sprinkle with the sifted confectioners'
sugar and serve cut into 10 wedges.

Fruity Filo Baskets

INGREDIENTS

4 sheets filo dough

10½ oz/300 g cooking apples, peeled, cored, and chopped

1 tbsp finely grated orange rind

1 tbsp maple syrup, or to taste

2 tbsp water

3 fresh mandarins, peeled and segmented

2 tbsp toasted slivered almonds or coconut flakes

1 Preheat the oven to 375°F/190°C. Place a sheet of dough on a clean counter and cut into 6 squares. Brush one piece lightly with water and place a second sheet on top. Brush again and repeat the layering using another 3 pieces. Keep the dough moist while doing this by covering with a clean damp cloth. Make 5 more layered filo piles in the same way.

2 Mold the 6 filo dough piles into 4-inch/ 10-cm ovenproof containers, such as muffin pans. Push the dough carefully into the bases to form baskets. Crumple a small sheet of foil into each to help keep their shape.

3 Bake for 8 to 10 minutes, or until crisp. Remove the foil and, if the bases are not crisp, return to the oven for 3 to 5 minutes. Remove from the oven and leave until cold.

4 Place the apples in a pan with the orange rind and maple syrup. Add the water, then cook gently for 8 to 10 minutes until tender. Cool a little, then beat until smooth. Leave until cold.

5 When ready to serve, spoon the prepared apple filling into the filo baskets and top with the mandarin segments. Sprinkle with the almonds or coconut flakes and serve.

5 Drinks

This chapter has something for everyone, from fruit smoothies, such as Peach or Apple & Raspberry to a refreshing glass of Fresh Lemonade. There is also a banana milkshake and even alcoholic drinks like the Summer Punch to help you relax and unwind at the end of a busy day.

Peach Smoothie

INGREDIENTS

serves 1
calories per
glass

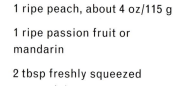
98

1 ripe peach, about 4 oz/115 g

1 ripe passion fruit or
mandarin

2 tbsp freshly squeezed
orange juice

3 tbsp lowfat plain yogurt

1 tsp honey (optional)

crushed ice

1 Cut the peach in half, discard the pit, and slice the flesh. Reserve 1–2 slices for decoration and place the rest in a smoothie machine or blender.

2 Scoop out the seeds from the passion fruit, if using, and add to the peach slices. If using a mandarin, peel and divide into segments and add to the peach. Switch on and, with the motor running, slowly pour in the orange juice and the yogurt. Add honey to taste, if using, and blend for 30 seconds, or until smooth.

3 Half-fill a tall glass with crushed ice and pour the smoothie over. Decorate with the reserved peach slice and serve immediately.

Carrot & Broccoli Juice

serves 1
calories per
glass

89

INGREDIENTS

1 carrot, about 2 oz/55 g, peeled and cut into small chunks

about 4 tbsp water

1 oz/25 g fresh tender broccoli florets

1 large orange, peeled and divided into segments

Worcestershire sauce, to taste

⅔ cup chilled mineral water

crushed ice

1 celery stalk

orange slice, to decorate

1 With the motor running in a smoothie machine or blender, drop in the carrot then pour in about 2 tablespoons of the water. Add the broccoli and another 2 tablespoons of water, then add the orange segments.

2 Add a few dashes of Worcestershire sauce and the chilled mineral water, and blend until smooth. Put some crushed ice into a tall glass and pour over the juice. Add a celery stalk for stirring, then decorate with an orange slice and serve.

Spicy Tomato & Orange Smoothie

INGREDIENTS

serves 1
calories per
glass

4 oz/115 g ripe tomatoes
(peeled if preferred),
coarsely chopped

2 scallions, trimmed
and chopped

⅔ cup orange juice

Tabasco sauce, to taste

crushed ice

chilled mineral water
(optional)

fresh basil sprig, to decorate

1 Put the tomatoes in a smoothie machine or blender. Switch on and with the motor running add the scallions and the orange juice to the tomatoes.

2 Add a few dashes of Tabasco sauce and continue to blend for 1 minute, or until smooth.

3 Half-fill a tall glass with crushed ice then pour over the juice. Top off with some chilled mineral water, if using, then decorate with a basil sprig and serve.

Apple & Raspberry Smoothie

serves 1
calories per
glass

93

INGREDIENTS

1 eating apple, peeled, cored, and chopped

2 tbsp chilled mineral water

2 oz/55 g fresh or thawed frozen raspberries

1 tsp honey (optional)

4 tbsp buttermilk or lowfat plain yogurt

ice cubes

1 Put the apple in a smoothie machine or blender together with the mineral water and blend for 1 minute.

2 Reserve 2–3 raspberries for decoration and add the rest to the smoothie machine. Blend for 30 seconds before adding the honey, if using, and then add the buttermilk. Blend for an additional minute.

3 Place a few ice cubes into a tall glass, pour over the smoothie, decorate with the reserved raspberries, and serve.

Fresh Lemonade

**serves 4
(5 cups/1.2
liters)**
calories per
1¼ cups

82

INGREDIENTS

3 ripe lemons (preferably organic or unwaxed)

heaping ½ cup superfine sugar, or to taste

4 cups boiling water

ice cubes

lemon slices, to decorate

1 Wash and thoroughly dry the lemons then, using a vegetable peeler, remove the rind from the lemons as thinly as possible. Set aside the lemons. Put the lemon rind into a heatproof bowl and sprinkle over the sugar. Pour over the boiling water, stir until the sugar has dissolved then cover loosely and leave until the liquid is cold.

2 Squeeze out all the juice from the lemons and pour into the cooled lemonade. Strain into a pitcher, check the sweetness, and add a little more sugar if required.

3 Place some ice cubes in a tall glass, pour in the lemonade, and decorate with a lemon slice. Serve.

Raspberry Crush

serves 4
calories
per
1¼ cups

63

INGREDIENTS

10½ oz/300 g fresh or thawed frozen raspberries

4 tbsp orange juice

1–2 tsp honey, or to taste

crushed ice

1¼ cups club soda

4 scoops raspberry sherbet or frozen raspberry yogurt

1 Set aside a few raspberries for the decoration then put the remainder in a smoothie machine or blender. Switch on and with the motor running, add the orange juice and blend for 1 minute.

2 Add the honey to taste and blend for 20 seconds. Half-fill a tall glass with the crushed ice and top off with the soda. Place a scoop of raspberry sherbet or frozen yogurt on top and serve decorated with the reserved raspberries.

Pineapple Crush

serves 4
calories
per 1¼ cups

52

INGREDIENTS

½ small ripe pineapple
(to give 8 oz/225 g of fresh
peeled pineapple)

2–3 tsp maple syrup, or to
taste

⅔ cup orange juice

2 tsp ground ginger, or to taste

crushed ice

1¼ cups American ginger ale
or chilled mineral water

8 long chives

1 Place the pineapple on a cutting board and cut away the plume, skin, and the base. Cut the pineapple into quarters and cut away the hard central core. Chop the flesh into small pieces.

2 Place a few pieces of pineapple in a smoothie machine or blender and blend for 1 minute. Add the maple syrup and about ¼ cup orange juice. With the motor running, add the remaining pineapple, a few pieces at a time, with a little more orange juice.

3 When all the pineapple and juice have been used, add the ground ginger and blend again briefly. Place some crushed ice in tall glasses and fill with the pineapple juice. Top off with ginger ale, decorate with 2 chive lengths per glass, and serve.

Lowfat Banana Shake

INGREDIENTS

serves 1
calories per
portion

86

2 oz/55 g ripe bananas, peeled and cut into chunks

1 tsp maple syrup, or to taste

1 tsp ground cinnamon (optional)

⅔ cup lowfat milk

crushed ice

1 scoop lowfat vanilla or chocolate ice cream

sprinkle of grated chocolate (optional)

1 Put the banana chunks in a smoothie machine or blender, with the maple syrup, to taste, and the ground cinnamon, if using. Switch on and with the motor running, add the milk and blend for 1 minute, or until smooth.

2 Place some crushed ice in a tall glass and pour the shake over. Add a scoop of lowfat vanilla or chocolate ice cream and serve sprinkled with a little grated chocolate, if using.

Summer Punch

serves 10
calories
per ⅔ cup
glass

INGREDIENTS

75 cl bottle rosé wine, chilled

1 tbsp honey

⅔ cup brandy (optional)

4 oz/115 g mixed summer
berries, such as raspberries,
blueberries, and strawberries

3–4 fresh mint sprigs

2½ cups chilled sparkling
water

8 ice cubes

1 Pour the wine into a punch bowl or large
glass serving bowl. Add the honey and stir
well, then add the brandy, if using.

2 Cut any large fruits into bite-size pieces
and place all the fruits and mint sprigs into
the wine.

3 Let stand for 15 minutes then add the
sparkling water and the ice cubes. Ladle the
punch into glasses or punch cups ensuring
each has an ice cube and a few pieces of fruit.
Serve with a spoon to eat the fruit, if using.

Winter Warmer

serves 10
calories
per ⅔ glass

INGREDIENTS

75 cl bottle red wine, such
as claret

heaping ¼ cup light soft brown
sugar

2 bruised cinnamon sticks,
plus extra unbruised cinnamon
sticks, to decorate (optional)

1 tsp allspice

4–6 whole cloves

1 small orange (preferably
organic or unwaxed)

1 lemon (preferably organic
or unwaxed)

⅔ cup rum or brandy

⅔ cup black tea,
made from Darjeeling tea

1 Pour the red wine into a heatproof bowl and
place over a pan of gently simmering water.
Add the sugar with all the spices.

2 Cut the orange and lemon into thin slices,
then add to the wine with the rum. Heat gent
stirring occasionally, for 15 to 20 minutes,
or until the sugar has dissolved and the wine
is hot.

3 Pour in the tea, heat for an additional
10 minutes, and then serve in heatproof
glasses. Decorate the glasses with extra
unbruised cinnamon sticks, if liked.

Index